HAL LEONARD

PIANO METHOD

PIANO FOR KIDS

A Beginner's Guide with Step-by-Step Instruction for Piano

BY JENNIFER LINN

To access audio visit:
www.halleonard.com/mylibrary

Enter Code
1843-3755-0713-9434

ISBN 978-1-4950-5942-1

7777 W. BLUEMOUND RD. P.O. BOX 13819 MILWAUKEE, WI 53213

Visit Hal Leonard Online at
www.halleonard.com

INTRODUCTION

Welcome to *Piano For Kids!* This book is for beginners who want to learn how to play the piano (or keyboard), and want to play the popular songs they know and love. Students will first begin to read music with pre-staff notation (note names are written inside each note) and then progress to reading music on the staff. Each new song builds on concepts they have learned in previous songs, so kids can progress with confidence. The audio tracks included with this book are a great teaching tool allowing kids to listen, learn, and play along! Let the joy of learning to play the piano begin!

–Jennifer Linn

ABOUT THE AUDIO

To access the accompanying audio, simply go to **www.halleonard.com/mylibrary** and enter the code found on page 1 of this book. This will grant you instant access to every file. You can download to your computer, tablet, or phone, or stream the audio live—and if your device has Flash, you can also use our *PLAYBACK+* multi-functional audio player to slow down or speed up the tempo, change keys, or set loop points. This feature is available exclusively from Hal Leonard and is included with the price of this book!

For technical support, please email support@halleonard.com

CONTENTS

WHAT KIND OF PIANO DO YOU HAVE?

You can play all the songs in this book with all the piano types shown on this page.

ACOUSTIC PIANOS

The term 'acoustic' is used to describe a piano that produces its sound naturally with felt-covered hammers striking wire strings made of steel. The acoustic piano (grand or upright) has a full keyboard with 88 keys.

Grand Piano

Upright (Vertical) Piano

DIGITAL (ELECTRONIC) PIANOS

The digital piano uses electronics to produce the piano sounds and various instrumental accompaniments depending on the model type.

Digital pianos are available with different keyboard sizes. While the smaller keyboards are sufficient for this book, keep in mind that a beginner may quickly outgrow the smaller keyboards and need a full size instrument.

61 keys

88 Keys (Full Size)

76 keys

PARTS OF THE PIANO

UPRIGHT PIANO

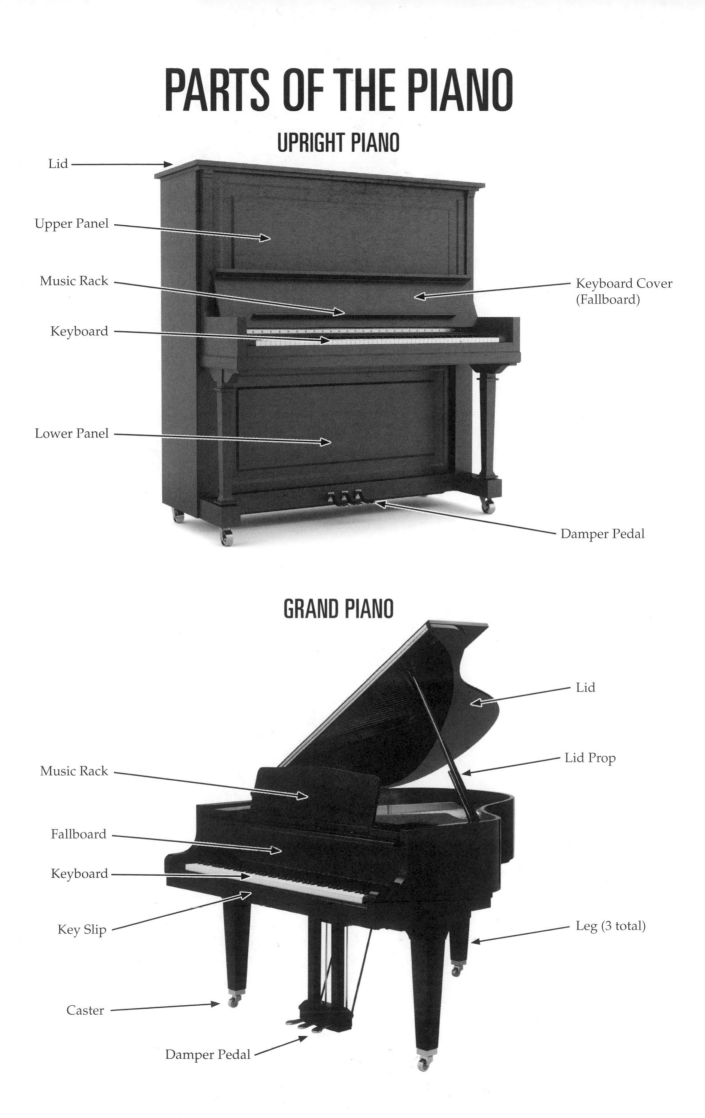

Lid

Upper Panel

Music Rack

Keyboard

Keyboard Cover
(Fallboard)

Lower Panel

Damper Pedal

GRAND PIANO

Music Rack

Fallboard

Keyboard

Key Slip

Caster

Damper Pedal

Lid

Lid Prop

Leg (3 total)

HOW TO SIT AT THE PIANO

- Sit tall on the front half of the bench.
- Lean slightly forward.
- Keep your feet flat on the floor.
- Your knees should be only slightly under the keys.
- Your elbows should be higher than the keyboard level.
- Keep your shoulders relaxed.

GOOD HAND POSITION

- Make sure your wrist and back of the hand form a straight line.
- Curve your fingers so that only your fingertips are touching the keys.
- Use the side tip of your thumb.
- Keep your wrist relaxed and flexible.

FINGER NUMBERS

- Each finger is assigned a number.
- Place your palms together with your fingertips touching.

  Tap 1's (thumbs)

  Tap 2's

  Tap 3's

  Tap 4's

  Tap 5's

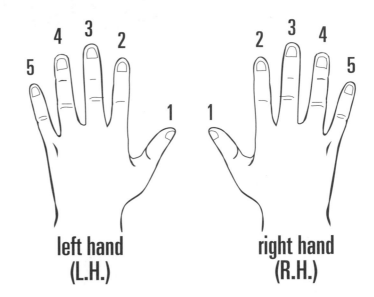

left hand
(L.H.)

right hand
(R.H.)

- FINGERING: The finger numbers will appear above and below the music notes. These numbers are known as the fingering and are to be followed exactly.

THE KEYBOARD

The keyboard consists of white and black keys. The black keys are arranged in groups of twos and threes.

- Circle all the 2 black-key groups and box all the 3 black-key groups below.

- Play all the 2 black-key groups on your keyboard with your L.H., using fingers 2 and 3.

- Play all the 3 black-key groups with your R.H., using fingers 2, 3, 4.

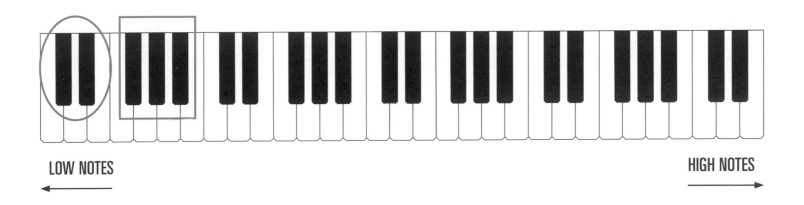

LOW NOTES

HIGH NOTES

RHYTHM IN MUSIC: QUARTER NOTE AND REST

Rhythm in music needs a steady **BEAT**. The quarter note gets one beat of sound and the quarter rest gets one beat of silence.

♩ = 1 beat of sound

𝄽 = 1 beat of silence

Place your R.H. and L.H. 2nd fingers on two white-key D's in the center of your keyboard. Think **"D for doghouse"** to help you remember.

Down stems are for L.H. notes.

Up stems are for R.H. notes.

L.H. 2   R.H. 2

FEEL THE BEAT
TRACK 1

R.H.
2

Feel the beat now! Keep it stead - y. Keep it go - ing 'til you're read - y.

2
L.H.

HICCUP RAP
TRACK 2

R.H.
2

UH OH! (hic) I think I (hic) just might (hic) have the (hic) hic - cups! (hic)

2
L.H.

THE HALF NOTE AND HALF REST

♩ = 2 beats of sound   ▬ = 2 beats of silence

BARLINES divide the music into **BARS**. Tap the rhythm below with your right hand on the closed lid. Remember that the quarter rest is one beat of silence and the half rest is two beats of silence.

WE WILL ROCK YOU

TRACK 3

Words and Music by Brian May

Play the first 4 bars again

Double Barline (end)

THE NOTES C D E

- You already know how to find D. The notes C and E are right next door!
- Place your R.H. thumb on middle C and play C D E with fingers 1, 2, 3.
- Now play it backwards (E D C) with fingers 3, 2, 1.
- Play all the C D E's on your keyboard.

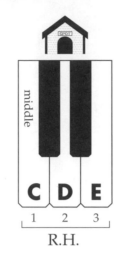

Remember to play the middle C with the side tip of your thumb and keep a rounded hand shape.

MARY'S BIG FROG

TRACK 4

Mar - y had a   big   frog,   big   frog,   big   frog.

Ev - 'ry - where that   frog hopped,   Mar - y   al - so   hopped too!

10

THE NOTES G AND A

- The 3 black-key group will help you find the G and A.
- With your L.H., "park" fingers 2 and 3 in the "double garage."
- Remember to play with curved fingers and a rounded hand shape.

TIME SIGNATURE

$\mathbf{4}$ = 4 beats per bar

$\mathbf{4}$ = ♩ gets one beat

The time signature tells how many beats are in a bar, and what kind of note gets one beat.

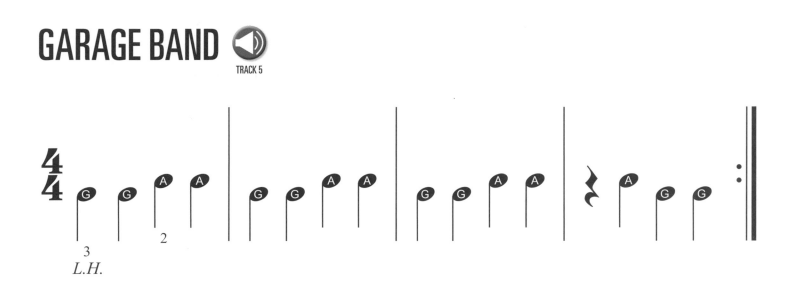

GARAGE BAND TRACK 5

HONKING HORNS TRACK 6

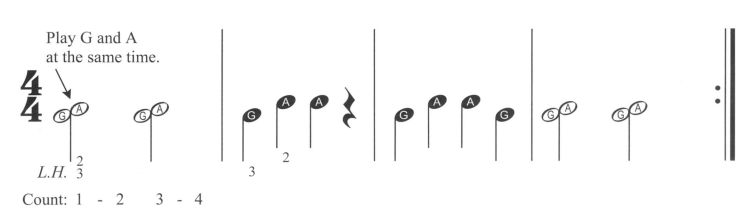

Count: 1 - 2   3 - 4

NEW NOTE B

WOLFGANG AMADEUS MOZART (1756–1791)

Mozart was a famous classical composer from Austria. He wrote a very popular piece for the piano based on the familiar tune "Twinkle, Twinkle, Little Star."

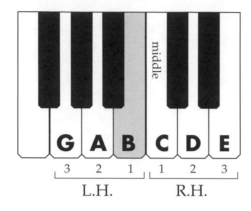

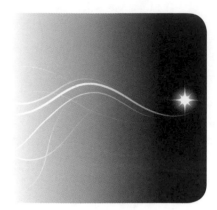

WARM-UP

- Place your L.H. thumb (1) on B, 2 on A, and 3 on G. Play **B A G** and **G A B**.
- Place your R.H. thumb (1) on C, 2 on D, and 3 on E. Play **C D E** and **E D C**.
- Now use both hands to play **G A B – C D E** and then play it backwards **E D C – B A G**.

MOZART'S TUNE

TRACK 7

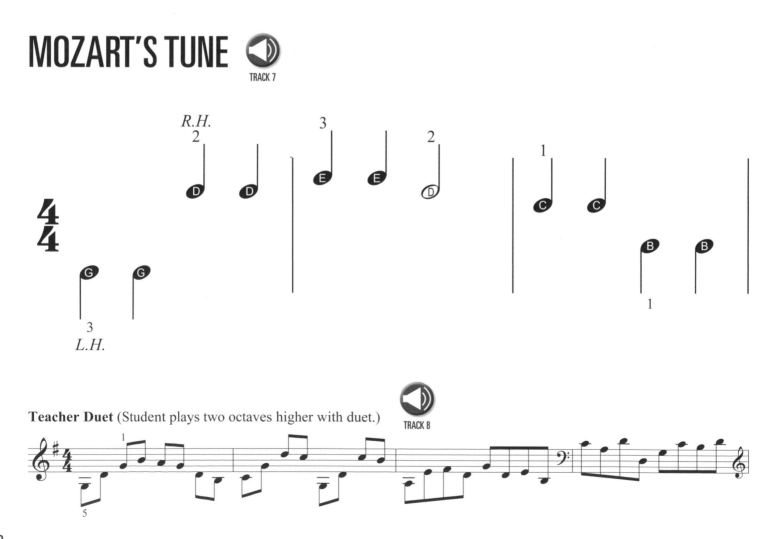

Teacher Duet (Student plays two octaves higher with duet.)

TRACK 8

NEW NOTES F AND G

= 3 beats

DOTTED HALF NOTE
Count: 1 - 2 - 3

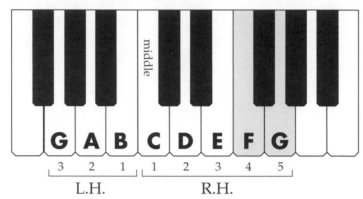

TIME SIGNATURE

3 = 3 beats per bar
4 = ♩ gets one beat

IN MY DREAMS
TRACK 9

Words and Music by
Jennifer Linn

Close to my heart, nev - er a - part,

(Count: 1 - 2 - 3)

Teacher Duet (Student plays two octaves higher with duet.) TRACK 10

pp
With pedal

14

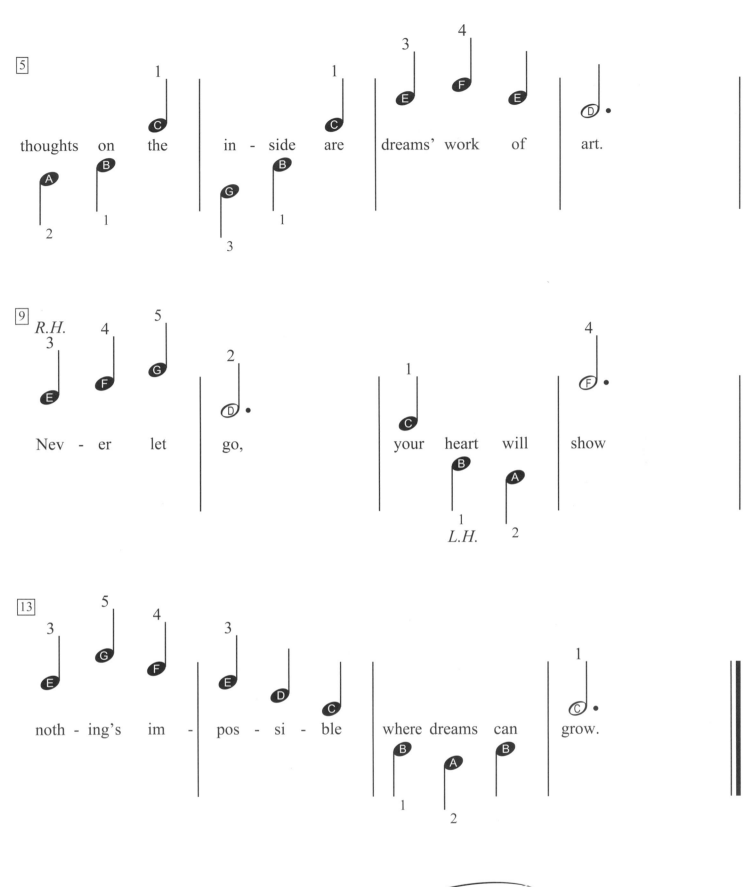

thoughts on the | in - side are | dreams' work of | art.

Nev - er let | go, | your heart will | show

noth - ing's im - | pos - si - ble | where dreams can | grow.

mp

poco rit.

WHOLE NOTE AND TIE

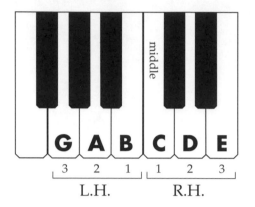

TIE

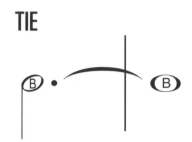

𝆰 = 4 beats

WHOLE NOTE

Count: 1 - 2 - 3 - 4

A **tie** joins two note values together. Hold the note for the total number of beats.

THE SIAMESE CAT SONG
from Walt Disney's LADY AND THE TRAMP

TRACK 11

Words and Music by Peggy Lee and Sonny Burke

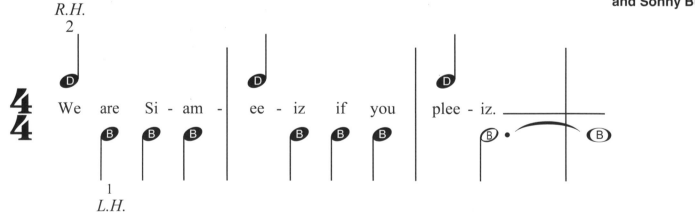

We are Si - am - ee - iz if you plee - iz.

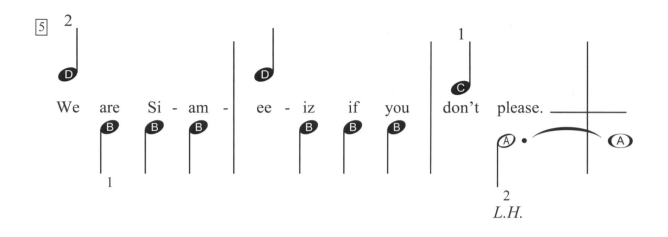

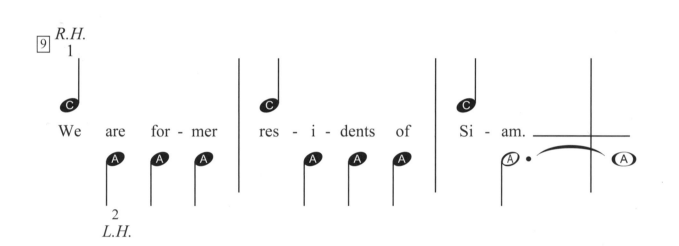

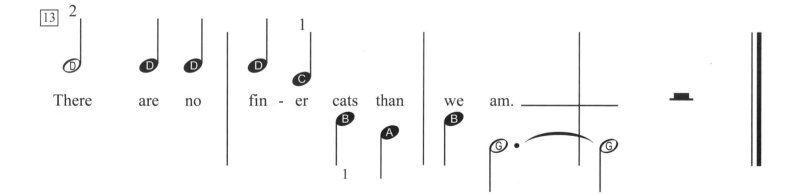

BEETHOVEN'S REVIEW

LUDWIG VAN BEETHOVEN
(1770–1827)

Beethoven was one of the greatest composers of all time. He wrote almost 400 compositions including this famous melody you will play from his Symphony No. 6 (Pastoral).

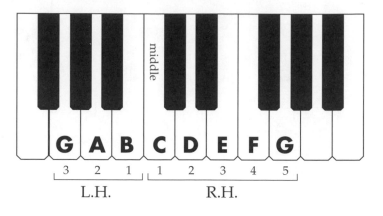

SYMPHONY NO. 6 (Pastoral)
(5th Movement)

TRACK 12

Ludwig van Beethoven

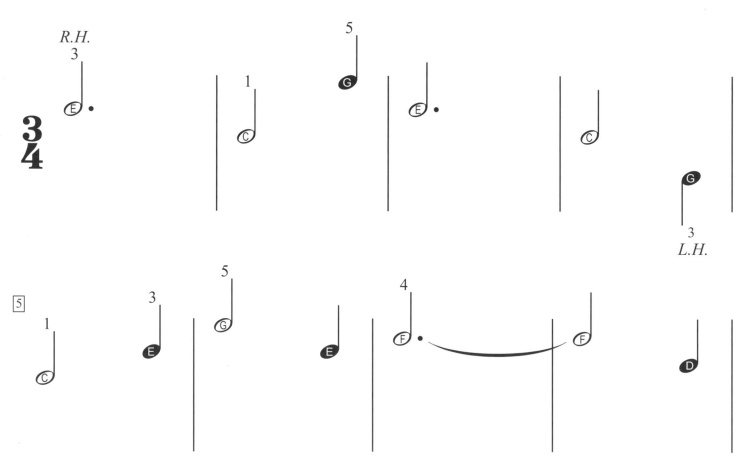

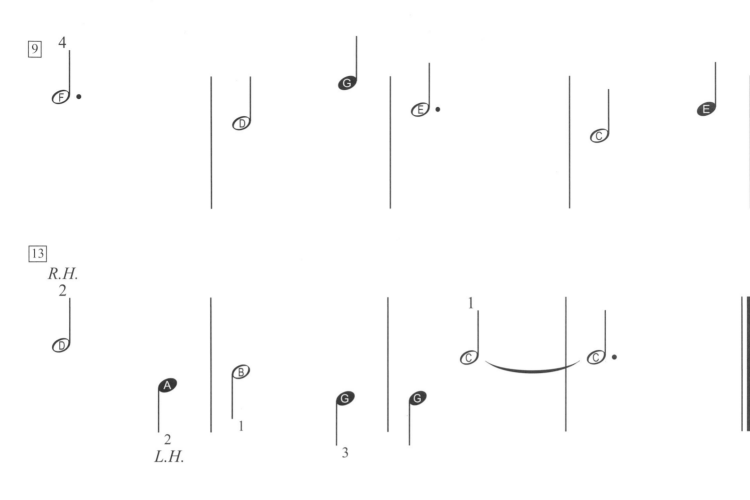

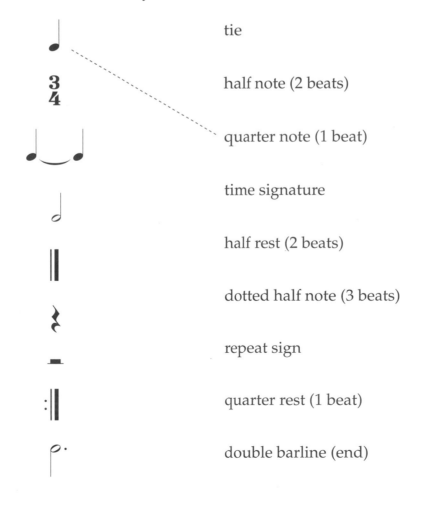

BEETHOVEN'S REVIEW MATCH

Draw a line to connect each musical symbol to its correct name.

tie

half note (2 beats)

quarter note (1 beat)

time signature

half rest (2 beats)

dotted half note (3 beats)

repeat sign

quarter rest (1 beat)

double barline (end)

DYNAMICS

Dynamic markings are symbols that tell you how loud or soft to play.

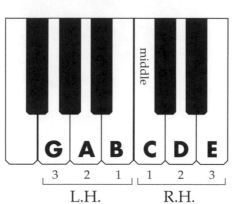

$\boldsymbol{p}$ = Soft (*piano*)

$\boldsymbol{f}$ = Loud (*forte*)

HALLELUJAH

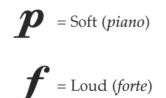

TRACK 13

**Words and Music by
Leonard Cohen**

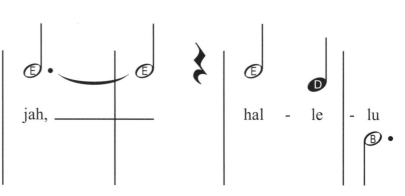

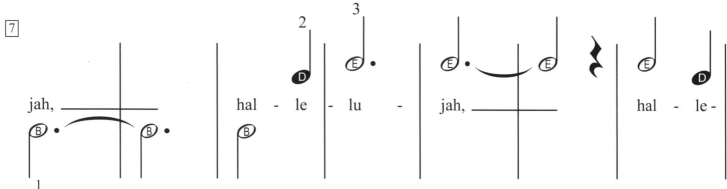

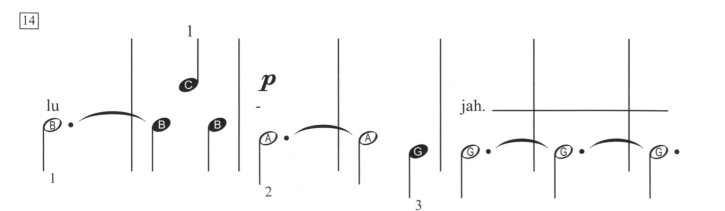

20

TWO EIGHTH NOTES

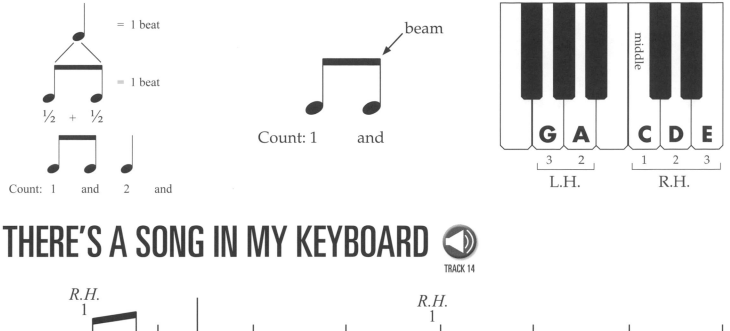

THERE'S A SONG IN MY KEYBOARD

TRACK 14

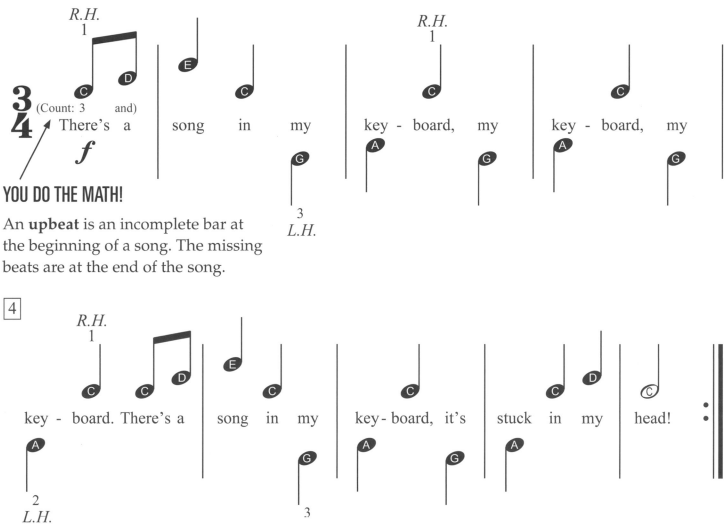

YOU DO THE MATH!

An **upbeat** is an incomplete bar at the beginning of a song. The missing beats are at the end of the song.

ADDITIONAL VERSES

VERSE 2:

Every time that I play it, I play it, I play it.
Every time that I play it, I play it again!

VERSE 3:

Have a headache, a headache, a headache a headache?
Have a headache, a headache, it's time to move on!

FERMATA

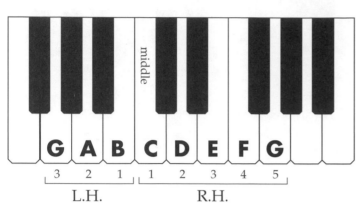

FERMATA

The **fermata** over a note tells you to hold the note a little longer.

HAPPY BIRTHDAY TO YOU

TRACK 15

Words and Music by Mildred J. Hill and Patty S. Hill

Teacher Duet (Student plays one octave higher.) TRACK 16

INTRODUCTION TO THE STAFF

STAFF

The **staff** is made with 5 lines and 4 spaces.

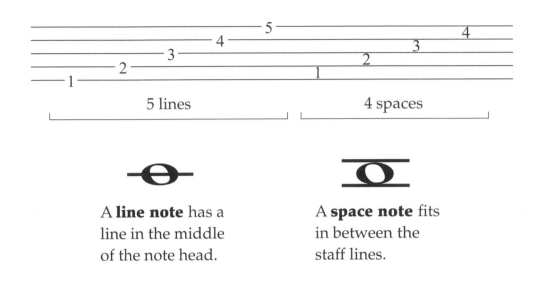

A **line note** has a line in the middle of the note head.

A **space note** fits in between the staff lines.

Write **L** for line note or **S** for space note in the blank below each note.

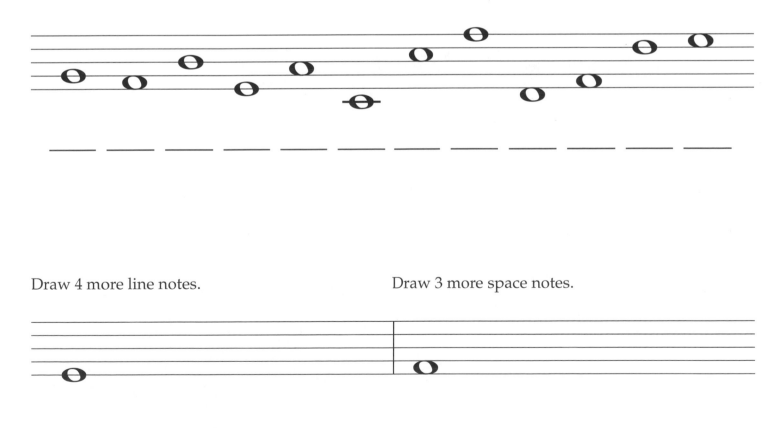

Draw 4 more line notes.

Draw 3 more space notes.

THE BASS AND TREBLE STAFF

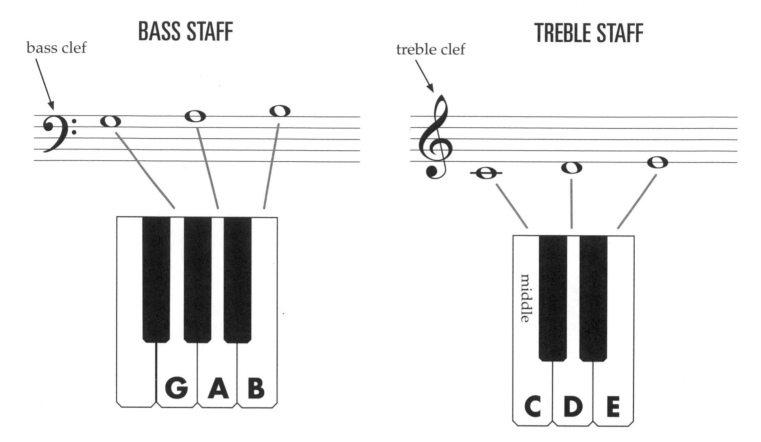

BASS STAFF

bass clef

G A B

TREBLE STAFF

treble clef

middle

C D E

In this book, the R.H. plays the treble staff notes and the L.H. plays the bass staff notes.

NOTE SPELLING CDE AND GAB

Write the correct **note name** in the blank below each note.

THE NOTES CDE ON THE STAFF

- Now you are ready to play the notes C, D and E while reading from the treble staff.
- Say the note names out loud as you play.

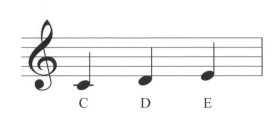

AU CLAIR DE LA LUNE  TRACK 17

French Folksong

HOT CROSS BUNS TRACK 18

Traditional

THE NOTES GAB ON THE STAFF

- Now you are ready to play the notes G, A and B while reading from the bass staff.
- Say the note names out loud as you play.

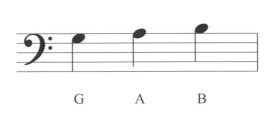

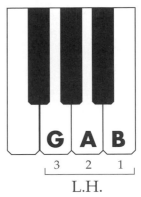

IN THE BAG
TRACK 19

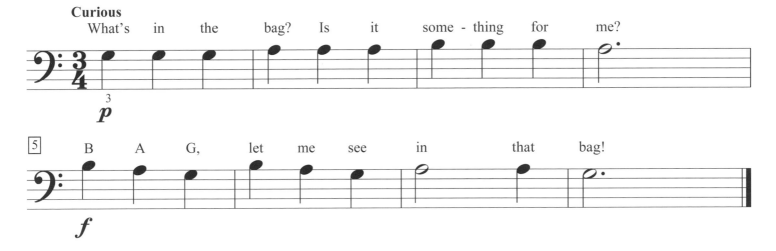

RHYTHM RAP
TRACK 20

Make up your own lyrics to "Rhythm Rap."

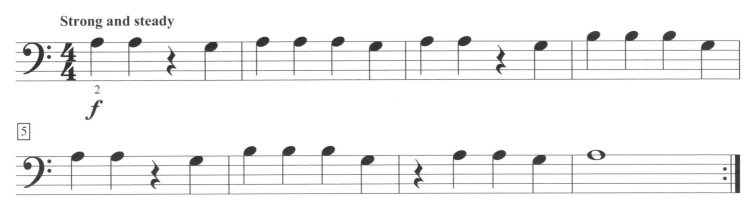

THE GRAND STAFF

The **grand staff** brings the treble staff and bass staff together. The staves are connected by a brace.

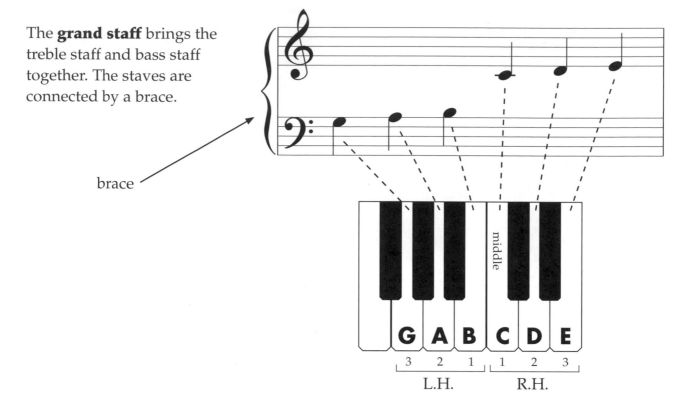

brace

Write the correct **note name** in the blank below each note to form words.

___ ___ ___   ___ ___   ___ ___ ___ ___

___ ___ ___ ___ ___   ___ ___ ___ ___

28

NEW DYNAMICS

$\textbf{\textit{mp}}$ = Medium soft (*mezzo piano*)

$\textbf{\textit{mf}}$ = Medium loud (*mezzo forte*)

MOZART ON STAGE

TRACK 21

WHOLE REST =
4 beats of silence

- Find the bar that is missing a whole rest and write in the rest.

- How many half rests are in this piece?

Note to teacher: May be played with the Teacher duet from "Mozart's Tune" on page 12.

F AND G ON THE STAFF

- Before you play "Can You Feel the Love Tonight," write the note name in the blank above each shaded note.

- Say the note names out loud as you play.

CAN YOU FEEL THE LOVE TONIGHT
from Walt Disney Pictures' THE LION KING

TRACK 22

Music by Elton John
Lyrics by Tim Rice

Moderately slow

Can you feel ____ the love ____ to - night? ____

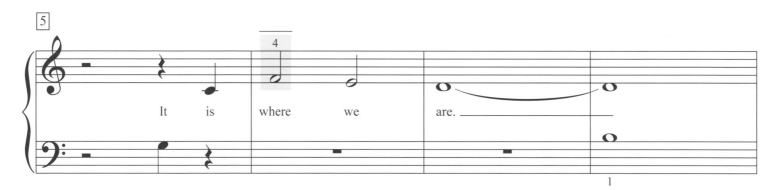

It is where we are. ____

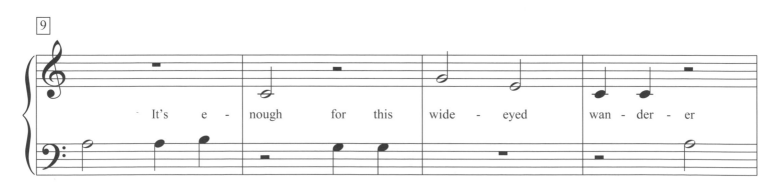

It's e - nough for this wide - eyed wan - der - er

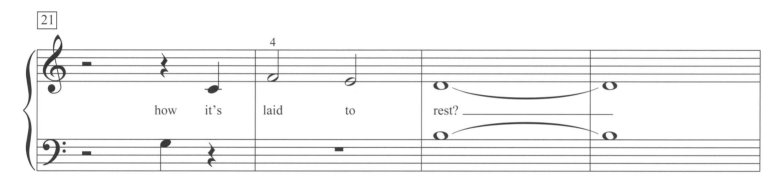

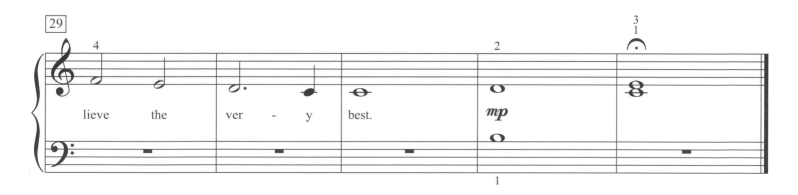

LEGATO, STACCATO AND SLUR

Legato means to play smoothly, without any gaps between the notes.

A dot under (or over) a note means to play the note **staccato**. To play **staccato**, release the key immediately, letting your wrist bounce slightly.

staccato dot

A **slur** over or under the notes means you play them **legato** (smoothly connected).

Remember: A tie might look the same as a slur, but the tie joins two identical notes.

How many ties are in "This Land Is Your Land"? _____

How many slurs? _____

THIS LAND IS YOUR LAND
TRACK 23

Words and Music by
Woody Guthrie

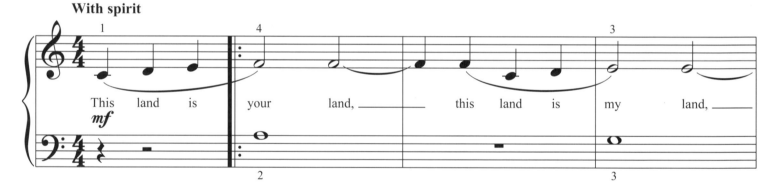

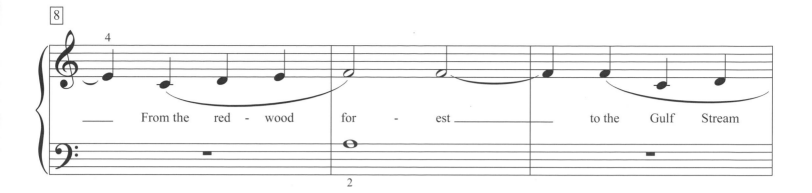

From the red - wood for - est _____ to the Gulf Stream

wa - ters, _____ This land was made for you and

1. Play 1st time only.

me.

As I was

2. Play 2nd time only.

me. _____

ADDITIONAL VERSES

As I was walking,
that ribbon of highway,
I saw above me
that endless skyway.
I saw below me
that golden valley,
This land was made for
you and me.

I've roamed and rambled
and I followed my footsteps
Through the sparkling sands of
her diamond deserts.
All around me,
a voice was sounding,
"This land was made for you
and me."

When the sun comes shining
as I was strolling,
the wheatfields waving
and the dust clouds rolling,
a voice was chanting
as the fog was lifting,
"This land was made for you
and me."

SHARING MIDDLE C

NEW L.H. POSITION

Your L.H. thumb will share middle C with your R.H. thumb. Your thumbs will take turns playing the exact same key.

Practice the exercise below. The thumb that is **not** playing should **make room** for the thumb that **is** playing. Do not use both thumbs at the same time.

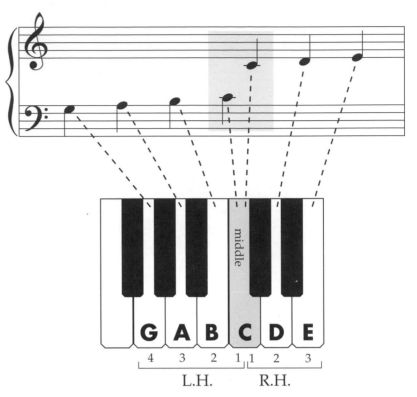

SHARING MIDDLE C

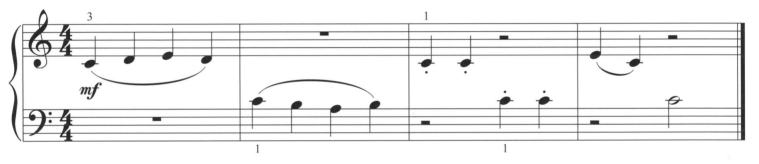

LET IT GO
from Disney's Animated Feature FROZEN

TRACK 24

Music and Lyrics by
Kristen Anderson-Lopez
and Robert Lopez

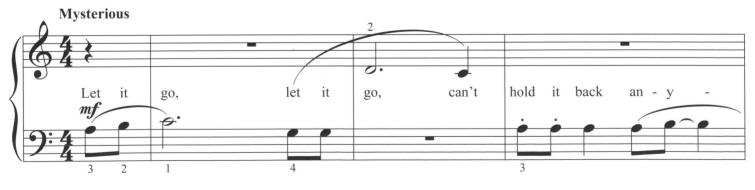

Let it go, let it go, can't hold it back an-y-

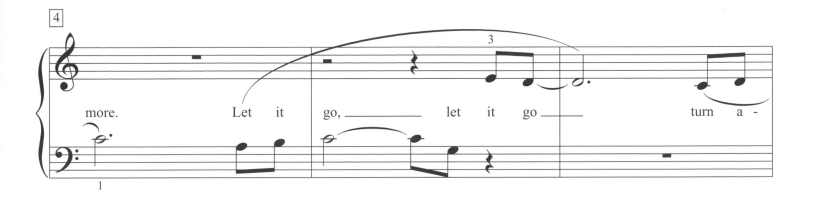

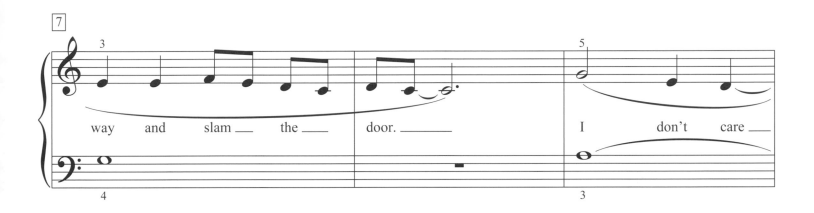

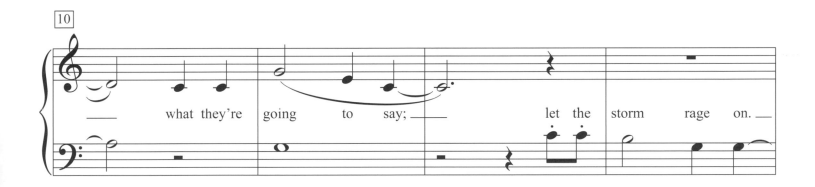

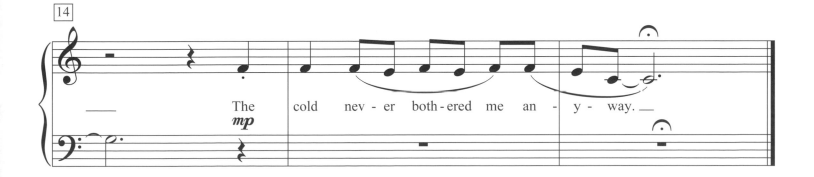

BASS NOTES E AND F

HAND POSITION SHIFT

In this book, when you see a fingering in a shading triangle, your hand will need to move higher or lower on the keyboard depending on the direction of the triangle.

E   F

- There are two new bass clef notes (E and F) in "Lean On Me." Fill in the rest of the note names above in the shaded boxes.

LEAN ON ME
TRACK 25

Words and Music by
Bill Withers

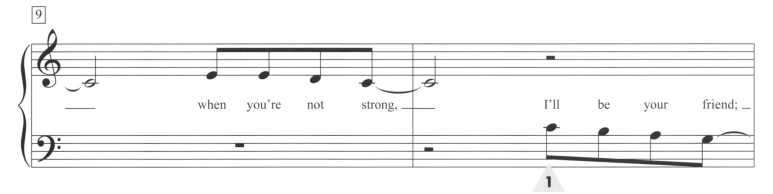

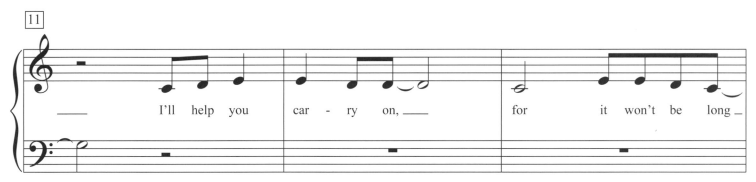

MARKS OF EXPRESSION

pp = Very soft (*pianissimo*)

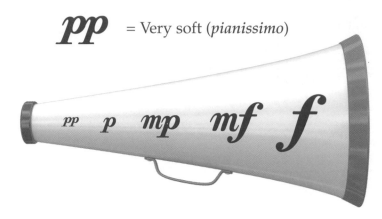

Crescendo means you play gradually louder.

Diminuendo means you play gradually softer.

BEAUTY AND THE BEAST
from Walt Disney's BEAUTY AND THE BEAST

TRACK 26

Music by Alan Menken
Lyrics by Howard Ashman

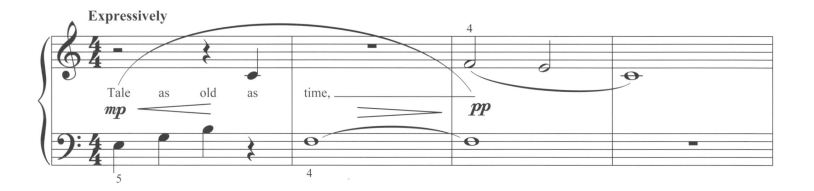

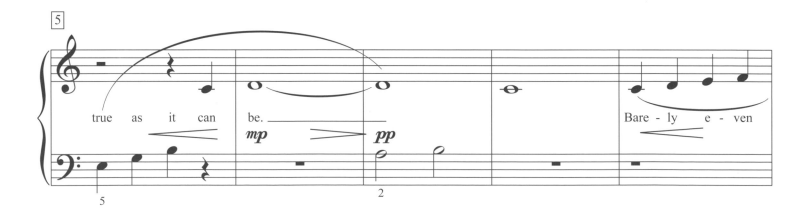

friends, then some-bod-y bends, un-ex-pect-ed-

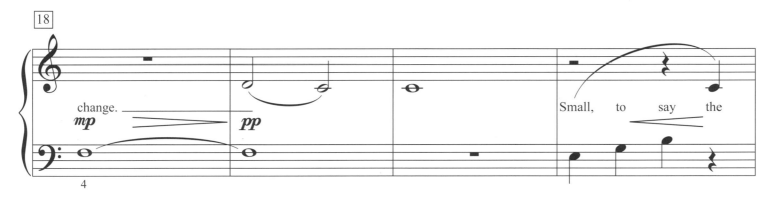

ly. Just a lit-tle

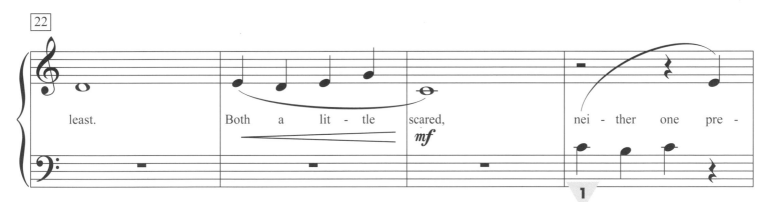

change. Small, to say the

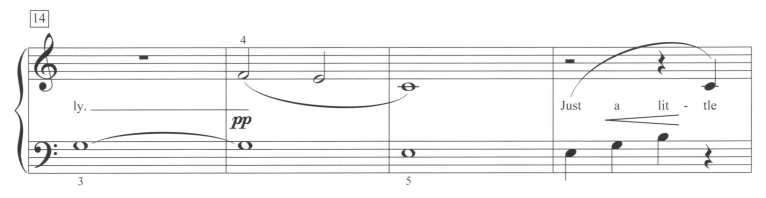

least. Both a lit-tle scared, nei-ther one pre-

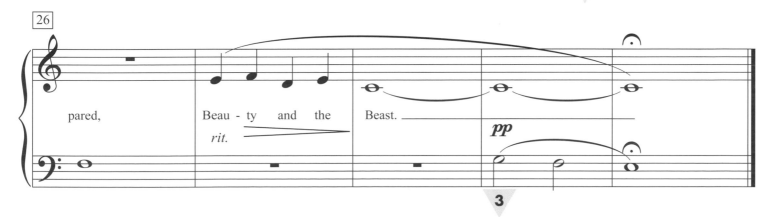

pared, Beau-ty and the Beast.

SHARPS

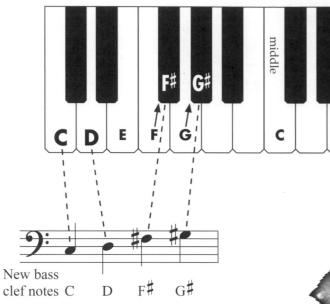

**SHARP**

A **sharp** sign before a note means to play the next key to the right. Once the sharp appears before a note, it remains sharp for the entire bar.

New bass
clef notes C   D   F#   G#

MY FAVORITE THINGS
from THE SOUND OF MUSIC

TRACK 27

Lyrics by Oscar Hammerstein II
Music by Richard Rodgers

With spirit

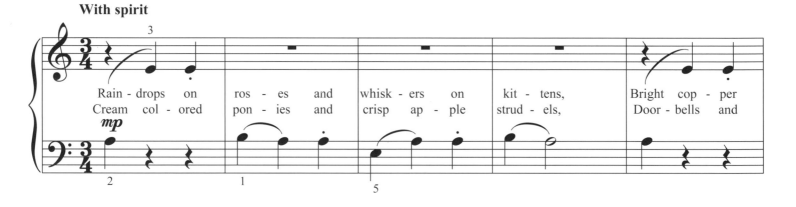

Rain - drops   on   ros - es   and   whisk - ers   on   kit - tens,   Bright cop - per
Cream col - ored   pon - ies   and   crisp ap - ple   strud - els,   Door - bells and

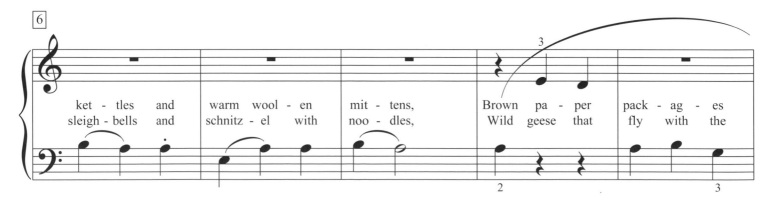

ket - tles   and   warm wool - en   mit - tens,   Brown pa - per   pack - ag - es
sleigh - bells and   schnitz - el   with   noo - dles,   Wild geese that   fly   with the

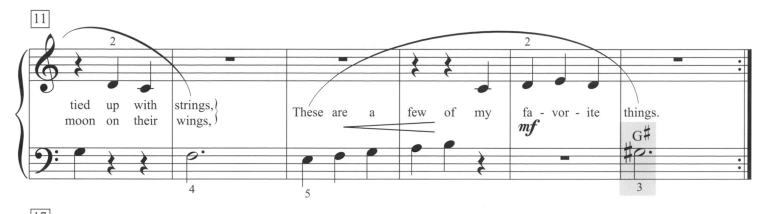

11

tied up with strings,
moon on their wings,)

These are a few of my fa - vor - ite things.

mf

G♯

17

Accent (Play note louder.)

When the dog bites, when the bee stings, when I'm

f

22

feel - ing sad, I sim - ply re - mem - ber my

mp

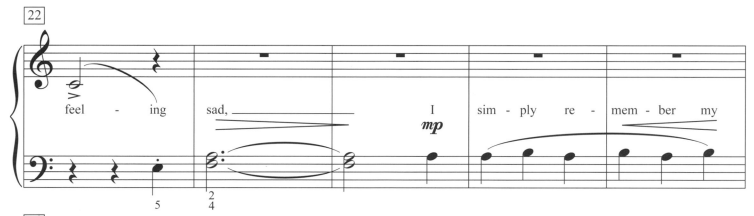

27

fa - vor - ite things, and then I don't feel

mf

A
F♯

(Stays F♯ because of the tie.)

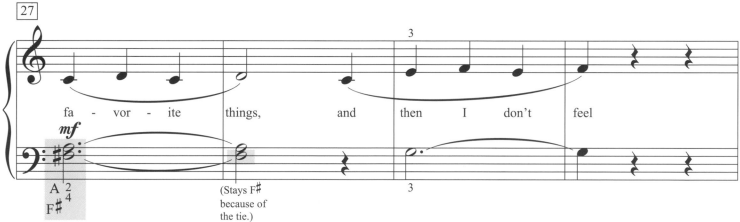

31

so bad.

f

Write the note names.

41

SINGLE EIGHTH NOTE AND REST

EIGHTH NOTE

♪ = 1/2 beat of sound

EIGHTH REST

𝄾 = 1/2 beat of silence

New R.H. treble clef notes

5   4   3
C   B   A

HEART AND SOUL
TRACK 28

from the Paramount Short Subject A SONG IS BORN

Music by Frank Loesser
Music by Hoagy Carmichael

With a bounce

mf

*Swing this rhythm by playing all ♫ "long-short."
Listen to the audio track to feel the beat.

Heart   and   soul,
Heart   and   soul,

I   fell   in   love   with   you.
I   beg   to   be a - dored.

the   way   a   fool would do,
and tum - bled o - ver - board,

Heart   and   soul,
Lost   con - trol

Count: 1   and   2   and   3   and   4

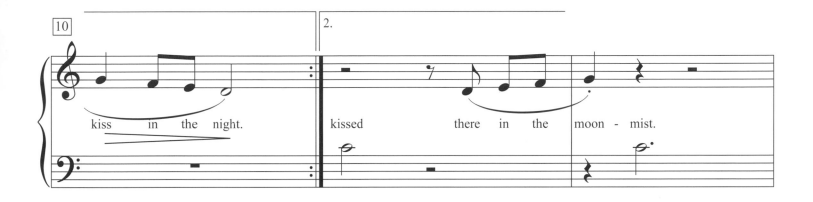

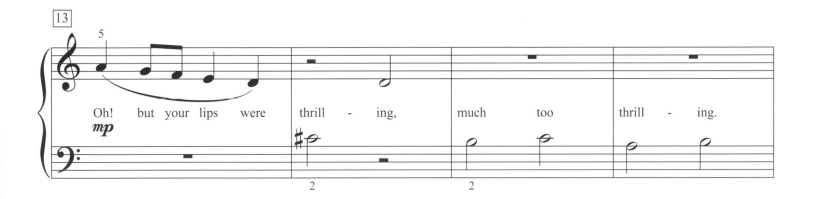

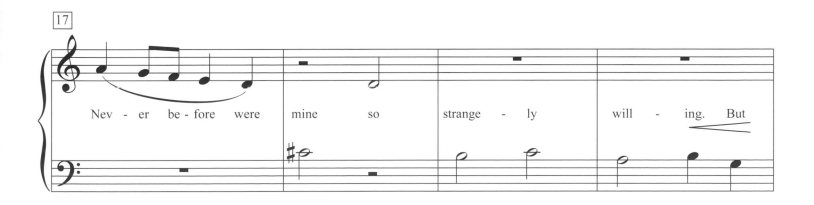

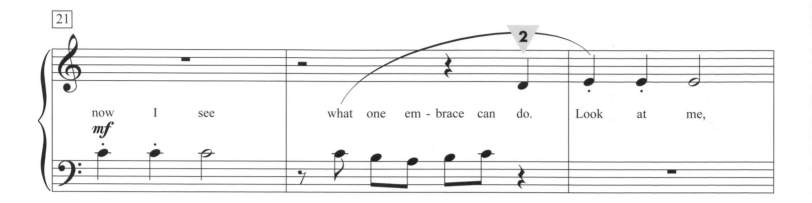

now   I   see   what one em - brace can do.   Look   at   me,

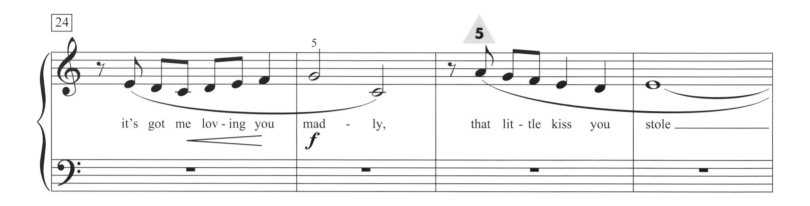

it's got me lov - ing you   mad - ly,   that lit - tle kiss you   stole _____

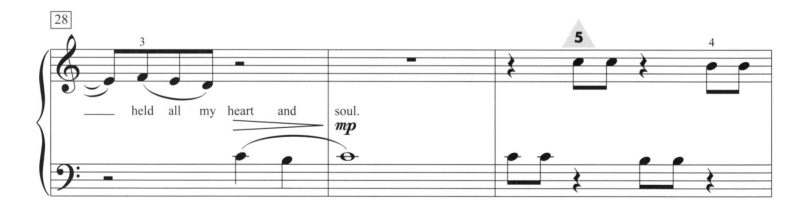

_____ held   all   my heart   and   soul.

FLATS

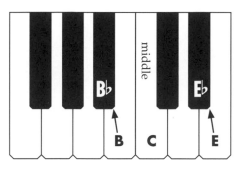

♭ FLAT

A **flat** sign before a note means to play the very next key to the left. Once the flat appears before a note, it remains flat for the entire bar.

DAMPER PEDAL MARKING

When you depress the **damper pedal** (right pedal) it lifts the dampers and allows the piano's strings to ring.

Pedal marking
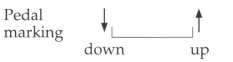
down   up

OVER THE RAINBOW
from THE WIZARD OF OZ

TRACK 29

Music by Harold Arlen
Lyric by E.Y. "Yip" Harburg

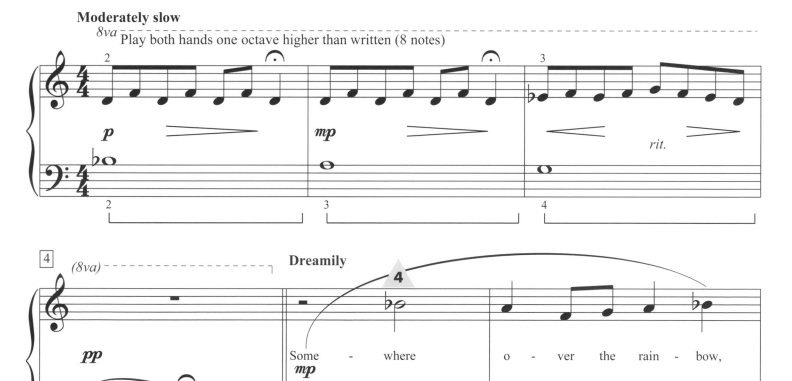

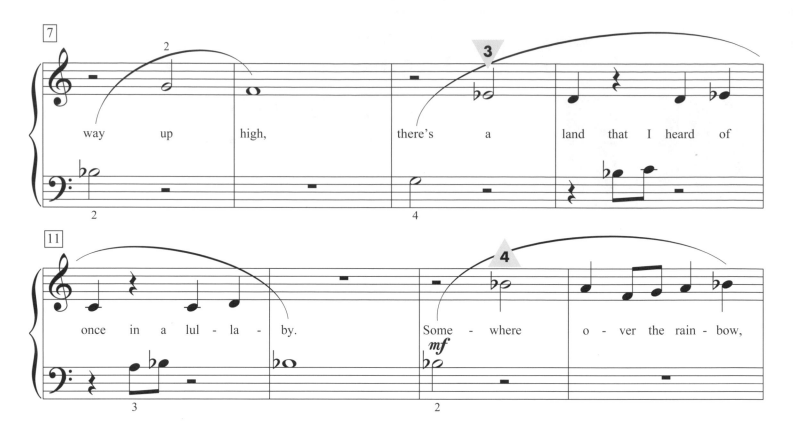

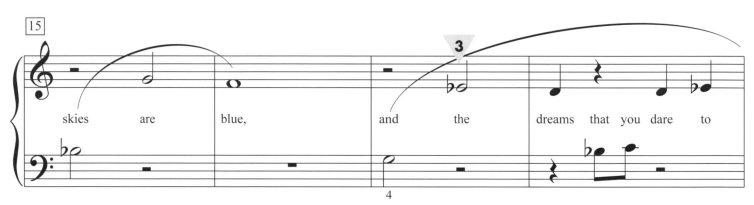

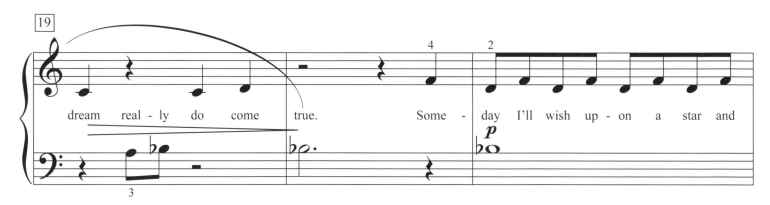

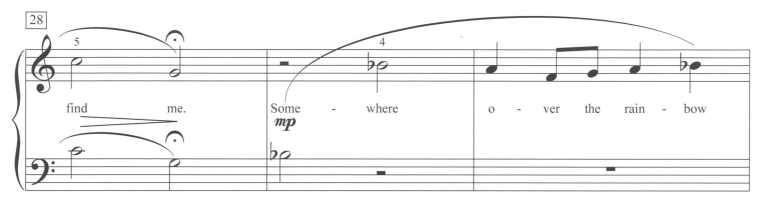

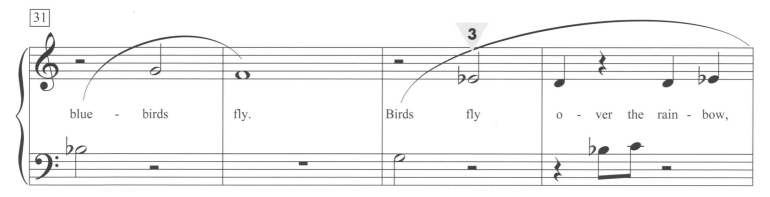

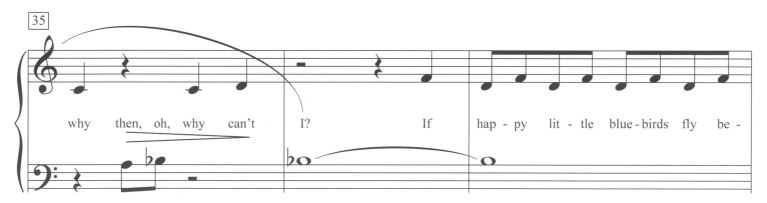

47

Certificate of Achievement

Congratulations to

_____
(YOUR NAME)

_____
(DATE)

You have completed

PIANO FOR KIDS

_____
(TEACHER SIGNATURE)

HAL•LEONARD®